Give or Take

Bernard Landreth

Red Squirrel Press

First published 2007 in the UK by Red Squirrel Press
PO BOX 219 MORPETH NE61 9AU
www.redsquirrelpress.com

Cover design by Mark Landreth

ISBN   978-0-9554027-0-8

Printed in the UK by Athenaeum Press Ltd.
Gateshead, Tyne & Wear

Acknowledgements

Pauline Plummer, Valerie Laws, BBC Radio, Blinking Eye Publishing, New Writing North, Northumbria University, Not Many Left, Ouse Valley Poetry Competition, PHRAS Poetry Competition, Poetry Life.

Contents

1

Arousal

I wake –
hot, unfocused
and primed for fathering.

Memory is downloaded in an instant:
my wife lies huge and taut –
a curl of hair, damp against her temple,
tells of an uneasy night
but she is sleeping now.

Our son has maggotted himself between us:
only night-dress, skin and tissue
separate his innocent small foot
from the sibling curled beyond his comprehension.

I watch my two loves sleeping:
instinct has positioned them
to calm their restlessness –
their faces almost touching,
each takes comfort from the other's breath.

Arousal is slow to accept its futility,
but I am content
in the gentle ache of unfulfilment.

At Mosedale

1

no child's metaphor
    he knows as no poet knows
        that hills touch the sky

2

a pure eager mind
    focused on the mystery
        of rabbit droppings

3

a cold mountain stream
    a fishing net and a splash:
        TROUT CATCHES SMALL BOY

Sunday Afternoon

Featureless cloud has dulled Thirlmere:
the water and the shrouded hills –
their colours deadened to sepia and grey –
lie as flat as a photograph.

He is trying to skim stones.

Only days before he was lying in a cylinder
as it banged and buzzed and formed
the images which will now have been developed
and filed for next week's appointment.

The cloud lifts like a dancer's veil.

The sun brightens the limbo of a Sunday afternoon:
colours the clearing high horizon,
paints the fleece of the tree-filled slopes
on the opposite shore with a thousand shades of green.

Light sparkles across the slight swell of the water.

A stone skips twice across the surface.
He turns in triumph – one small boy –
a foreground detail in an immense landscape.
I wave at him and clap.

He comes to sit beside me.

He is happy and untroubled
but I am isolated from him by my infectious fear.
Could love be more impotent?
All I have to give him is an apple and a can of pop.

A Solway Evening

They say love makes the world go round
but I had never felt it move
or seen it turn
until one Solway evening.

Across the low-tide estuary,
against the patterned red cliché
of a postcard sunset sky
the sun hung full and low.

Hypnotic, fierce, intense, unreal
and perfect as in animation
it coloured contoured hills
and stained the strands of sand and sea.

I stood alone, my son played trains
along the Silloth promenade,
too young to share my quiet game
which had no name or rules,

until he caught the burning sun
which scorched a strange unearthly sky:
it stopped him in his playful tracks –
he ran to hold my hand.

We watched it touch and slowly sink
as the cavemen and the Celt
through generations stood and watched
not comprehending what they saw.

Born to an age of comprehension
yet still seduced by their illusion,
I saw our circling source of light
closing another day.

Eight years old and full of learning
he clutched my hand in wonder
and as if it were a secret
whispered: *I can see the earth is moving.*

For Vacia

The tombstones of influential Romans
often included details of social rank,
careers, and personalised messages,
sometimes in the first person.

A child died as children often did.

As was the custom for a man of high rank,
the father commissioned a memorial
carved in stone with a girl holding grapes
and inscribed:
D   I   S
VACIA / INF
ANS / N III

The stone survived to stand
as an exhibit with others
(Titullinia Pussitta of Raetia
and Flavius Antigonus Papias,
a Christian and a citizen of Greece).

The museum's interpretation reads:
To the spirits of the departed
Vacia
an infant
aged 3

I hear a proud young Roman voice:
I am Vacia
I lived for three years
I learned to walk
I giggled
I sucked my thumb.

Fourteen

a schoolgirl standing at the edge

across the street three boys
make ludicrous adolescent angles
against the barriers
and try to generate enough saliva
for a spit

the lights change
the traffic parts for her

she steps onto the catwalk

Ripples

time to sit
a pebble in my hand
warm and smooth
as the sleeping sea it will disturb

plip

a small impertinence
gently tempered by the massive stillness

the metaphor is not the sea
and even the pebble
has more permanence than me

the ripples spread and fade

Carrock Fell

Always there,
beyond the garden and the fields:

sometimes dissolved
in mist or haze,

sometimes stretched out
below an ordinary sky,

sometimes white and bright
against a winter sky,

sometimes as distant
as in a watercolour,

sometimes so close
that I can see its texture and its contours.

On those best of days,
when it defies its distance
to rise like a feature on a huge relief map,
like the perfect diorama of an expert modeller,
it can startle me into belief.

On bad days
I don't even notice it.

Spring

The sun is getting up earlier than I am,
has coaxed the bulbs
to rise and set a good example.

Oystercatchers pose in pairs on motorway embankments,
a curlew calls across the moors,
chiffchaffs will soon be here.

Hope and optimism are knocking at my door,
but my life is so untidy I cannot let them in.

Caught

You should not have come,
but he was so eager
and the day is perfect.

The sickness has gone,
for the first time in three days
you have eaten some breakfast,
but staring down at the picnic
a familiar pain stabs you
with awful inevitability.

Shame has already wet your face
as he hands you a box of tissues from the car
and you run away from him across the heather.

Squatting behind the meagre cover
of a bed of bracken,
consumed by misery and humiliation,
wishing to be dissolved forever
into the Scottish landscape,
you cannot know
that sitting helplessly beside the sandwiches,
your new man
is suddenly overwhelmed by love.

I Love You: Define and Discuss

I love you:
>   my passwords to some heavy petting
>>   and her excuse for letting me go so far;
>   a simple phrase to label new, indescribable feelings;
>   the only words that matter.

And what potent words:
>   so powerful on the lips of a practised lover;
>   so persuasive as a plea for forgiveness;
>   so sustaining in separation – a message
>>   on a card or answerphone;
>   so breathtaking when spontaneous
>>   and unexpected.

But with time what routine words they can become:
>   as excuse or apology;
>   at the prompting of lust
>>   or as a reflex response to its fulfilment;
>   as the cruel prefix to a statement starting: *but*;
>   as a lazy, ineffective antidote to hurt.

And, if corrupted by a lifetime of misuse;
>   if stripped of all their meaning by mindless repetition;
>   what empty words they are:
>   a clichéd catchphrase
>   or one stale line from a tired old script.

But who needs words:
>   I have seen it in a smile;
>   I have shared it through an easy silence;
>   it's what I feel when I tap my fist
>>   against my best friend's arm
>>   and say: *Good to see you, Mate*;

what I have never said to any of the people
who have shown me how to love,
except one Sunday afternoon
when my emotions tripped
and I received an unenthusiastic hug
and a look which told me:
Dad, you're so embarrassing!

Climbing Helvellyn

Cagouled against the forecast rain,
up early to avoid the crowds,
they find familiar paths again
and climb towards the clouds.

Exertion takes their words away,
they struggle on neglected limbs –
too young for SAGA holidays,
too old for high-tech gyms.

Pausing below the hanging mist,
both knowing that they're just halfway,
unsure how tired the other is
but both too proud to say:

Let's stop – afraid of being the one
to end their annual pilgrimage
they joke and urge each other on
and onto Striding Edge.

In drizzle at the cairn they share
relief, exhaustion, memories –
old Wainwright, friend and guide, is there
to sketch what they cannot see.

They're back to Pooley Bridge by one
for Sunday lunch and Jennings beer,
their mutual smiles say: Well Done –
fit for another year.

A Small Memory

You lie on my arm – a stranger's arm –
delicate, trusting and warm;
contentedly fisting the air, then calmly
stretching a huge little yawn,
fists open in tiny perfection,
eyes close on a coarse sleeve bed
where in sleepily seeking protection
from me you give life to emotions long dead.

The instincts of parenthood, memories of birth
are revived by your quick gentle breathing.
Through your innocence God or this old godless earth
(whichever you grow to believe in)
shows the value of life and of each life the same –
an equality that you share with me
as my coffee turns cold and I trim fix and frame
this wonderful moment you give me.

Past's mirror reflects life's great memories –
birth and death, love and pain, joy and fear,
the moments of loss or discovery –
as images vast and unclear,
but small moments leave perfect reflections
which will never be dimmed or deform:
I save only the best in the private collection
where I now hang your six-week-old yawn.

Small Talk

Coffee and chocolates have been served,
the conversation adjourns to the lounge:
...the scenery was unbelievable...
...I love those prints...
...did you really?...

This is social grooming
by primates with no nits or fleas to pick:
we gather after feeding
and use 30,000 word vocabularies
to articulate our grunts.

Ashes

Behind ranks of relatives of 'The Deceased' –
a lampshade hat, a dandruffy parting –
I rise with the rest with the arms of the priest:
Let us pray *Our Auntie who art in* –
a coffin, recovering from God's sick joke
(reclaiming the soul from a body still living);
uneasy emotions are stirring, provoked
by Our Father's sin which we should be forgiving.

The priest is maudlin as an afternoon drunk,
he gushes an off-the-shelf epitaph,
before: ashes to ashes – *Major Tom is a junkie* –
a nail stabs my palm as I try not to laugh.

Then it's fish paste sandwiches, small sausage rolls,
'Cup of tea, dear? *Hope I die before I get old.*

Earth

death has turned fresh earth
        mourners hear a robin sing
                as it waits to feed

Dust

(after 'Memory' by John Clare)

Possessions will survive you when you die –
those things not sold at auction, lot by lot.
They won't be buried with you where you lie,
like treasure with a stone to mark the spot.
He'll know that some are his, though you forgot
to say so in your will, while she may sigh:
'I have such memories', and even weep
(but tears won't blur her keen collector's eye).

When fate or God decides my end is nigh,
when eyes close for that peaceful final sleep,
my hope is that I'll be surrounded by
possessions that no-one will want to keep:
that all my things and I will end our years,
them in a skip, me buried without tears.

2

The Birthday Waltz

His tie is knotted like a cravat,
he has combed his hair but forgotten his dentures:
still half-asleep from his afternoon nap
he's surprisingly active for his age and dementia.

There's a girl who looks just like Vivienne Leigh
and she's waiting for him in an evening gown
for a birthday dance (though it's afternoon tea,
in her wheelchair, in the residents' lounge).

But his smile cannot touch the skull-like face
of a body too old to clothe its bones
which mouths the cake with no sense of taste,
in the resident's lounge of the nursing home.

She is somewhere else or nowhere at all;
a pretty young carer wipes crumbs from her lips
as skeleton fingers pluck at the shawl
and then fend off the cup after two tepid sips.

One mind disconnected and one in free fall
which has caught on the ledge of an old memory:
a young man must dance with his girl at the ball
before he can sit for his afternoon tea.

He kisses her, sings *Happy Birthday to you*
as he slowly wheels her round the room.
No-one else sings, they never do –
it's her birthday every afternoon.

The Market Square

His orders were: advance and fire at will.
Terror gripped him, brought him to his knees.
He spat and wiped the vomit from his nose –
alone behind a low shell-blasted wall.

Smoke from a burning vehicle stung his eyes –
obscured the square. Immobilised by fear
he flinched at every round of mortar fire.
God knows which ones were theirs and which were ours.

I'd stopped behind a wall to have a shit.
A sergeant caught me there, dumping my load,
said, 'what the hell you doing, bonny lad,
hanging your bleeding arse out to get shot.

Don't wait for me to wipe it, move along!'
He saw the sergeant run ahead, then fall,
crawled forward through the smoke to where he fell.
The bullet must have ripped right through a lung.

He knelt and stared, not knowing what to do.
The sergeant lay there choking on his blood.
He tried a field dressing – still it bled.
He turned away and prayed for him to die.

He points: *You see the fountain in the middle?*
That's where a piece of shrapnel smashed my knee.
Sedated, it was days before he knew
he'd lost his leg. On crutches, with a medal,

they sent him home to months of being nursed,
then alcohol and anger, dreams and tremors.
Sometimes he wept – but no-one called it trauma.
For years I suffered badly with my nerves.

The square is bright and busy with a market
and crowded tables outside small cafés.
He lights a cigarette and sips his coffee.
That little Geordie sergeant didn't make it.

Spiderman

that's what she calls me
the home help
she's black
called Carol
it sounds a nicer name the way she says it

she says she's never known so many spiders
in one house
my pets she calls them
because I ask her not to kill them

she says I ought to get a proper pet
like a budgie
I tell her I don't like seeing birds in cages
she says *where else would you keep a budgie?*

she complains about the cobwebs
and the high ceilings where they hang
she has to clear them with a broom
she has a nice way of complaining

she says *damn spiders*
but today she helps me down on to my knees
so I that can rescue one
that is trapped inside the bath

she says *it won't help you if you get stuck in there*

she thinks I ought to move to sheltered housing

I say *neither would a budgie*

3

The Story So Far

Sometime between the big bang
and this Wednesday afternoon
it started with the animation of single cells.

Now there are billions of billion-celled beings –
specifically here in the park:
two walking each other around the boating lake,
one with a bag of the other's excreta;
some honking, recycling grass into green semi-liquid;
some hiding and seeking up and down tree trunks;
some stopping and starting over the putting green
listening for some which are moving beneath it;
some killing and eating;
some dying and being digested;
some nesting;
some messing around after school.

And amongst it all, with primal slime
still smeared across its cheeks,
evolution's latest model escapes its pushchair
to trample on the crocuses.

And above it all the trees live their rooted lives
unhindered by instincts and digestive systems.

City Weasel

Beyond the stone drain trench,
between the fences toeing and topping the bank,
separating car-packed concrete carriageways
from car-parked tarmac streets of terraced suburbs,
is a world without and formed from the debris of
humanity.

Seen only by jammed-up drivers,
a cast-off unkempt land of waste – rusting and broken,
a bonfired patch, bramble boughs, self-set shrubs,
willow herb and nettles, with stalks and sticks –
grey, dry and frail as fish bones
rising dead through the leaves, grass, scrap.

A wild side of the city
for the furred and feathered hunters
and the hunted – fearful, nesting unseen in tangles;
or buried, digging, scraping a furtive living;
or lower-living life which creeps, flits, flies,
dies never knowing fear.

Trapped in fuming unmoved traffic,
five o'clock headlines telling of life and death
in a world which is but often seems without
humanity, I saw it, tiny as a furry pet
but no pet this – pure carnivore –
its life is death.

Bright, chestnut, white-bellied;
sleek, supple and quick as a snake
it crossed the charred no-man's land
seeking cover like a seasoned soldier under fire,
a sniper, an assassin moving on his target.

A weasel, seen then out of sight in seconds,
moving from or to new death:
fertile egg or fledgling, mole or mousy rodent –
fresh food, warm flesh, life blood for a country killer
here making a city living.

In the Early Spring Air

Dry stone walls switchback the mounds
of the green rising land they divide into plots
where pipecleaner-leg lambs run in fear of the sound
of her laugh, to the ewes of a floor-mop flock.

Walking hand-out-of-hand, swapping light easy words,
we follow the path past some sparse stunted trees.
There's a far away ridge where a high preying bird
is circling the outcrops and steep slopes of scree.

She sits down to rest at an old stone wall stile
and leaves me with questions, what ifs and if onlys.
Has she been here before? With a lover? A child?
Do I make her feel happy and young? Or not lonely?

The words have all gone as I sit at her side
and she kicks at a tuft of the coarse spiky grass.
A curlew calls. She kicks and sighs
and I know that the moment won't last.

I finger the pattern which runs down her sleeve
and then she takes my hand and holds it to her breast:
as the rough lambs bully their mothers to feed
I can feel her heart racing beneath my caress,

but though warmed by her warmth to my hand, I'm aware
of my tense clumsy arms, of our middle-aged clothes,
of growing uncertainty in the early spring air
which chills me to shiver as my own heartbeat slows.

I search for assurance in her profiled face
as we sit on the cold polished knee of the stile
where she turns to adjust our awkward embrace,
releasing all doubt with a wonderful smile.

The sheep seem to mock me – *you're too old for this* –
but her eyes infuse youth through each numbed time-worn cell:
who cares – let the stupid sheep stare as we kiss
like shy teenage virgins on the cold unmoved fell.

Morecambe

At Morecambe on a spring bank holiday
they switch on flashing lights, beat disco drums
for lovely Lakeland hills across the bay.

Decked out in trinkets Blackpool threw away
the senile seafront opens shuttered slums
at Morecambe on a spring bank holiday.

Dad looks for bingo rooms where Gran can stay,
for family pubs, for young bikinied bums,
(for lovely Lakeland hills across the bay?)

Mum looks for kids; kids for expensive play
for which they plead and pester – she succumbs
at Morecambe on a spring bank holiday.

In brochure blurb for sand – read mud and clay;
for young and old – read anyone who comes;
for lovely Lakeland hills across the bay –

read hazy views. But here for just the day
what do they care – kids, dads and harassed mums
at Morecambe on a spring bank holiday,
for lovely Lakeland hills across the bay?

Players

She smiles in practised pose upon the couch,
will coyly sadden if I do not go
to sit and rest my head or kiss and touch,
will flush at my attention when I do.

Reclined her body lures me like the worm
a poacher casts and works to make his catch,
each movement matches mine as she performs,
each night my conscience begs me not to watch.

But as I push away her offered draught
and to her Siren play reluctant Clown,
desire fires temptation pleads: get caught,
as each urges the other be disowned.

How can a guilty heart pump shameless blood:
her hand rests on her thigh, it diagnoses
and then prescribes the treatment for my mood.
Why does my conscience fight – it always loses.

A voice cries out: *There must be more to this
than mime and guilt* – it brands me hypocrite.
Why am I here if not to touch and kiss?
My need is real, my guilt is counterfeit.

This is my lust, if that's all I aspire to
why draw her as a temptress, have I asked her
to script her own desires? Could I inspire her
to break out from the role in which I've cast her?

My cheated heart should not take second place
to balls, conned to produce what we don't need:
one half of life's great miracle debased –
a mess of eager unrequited seed

whose millions each seek substance as a child,
sustaining the obsession of my sex
with fucking, making nothing that's worthwhile
as I indulge it for its side effects.

Are we our genitals? Our minds, our souls
could touch, explore, create desire, achieve
some different climax, set some higher goal
than finding novel ways to not conceive.

But now the voice has had its futile rant,
her open smile and clothes will take their toll.
What better thing to do than what she wants,
I'll lie against her arm. I'll be her doll.

A stage, a lifeless manikin, the show
begins, I rise on cue, I touch her mouth:
but as we kiss the taste is sweeter now
than ever I remember in my youth.

So damn the voice and let my conscience rave –
the time for taunts and heckling is over;
how many men must yearn for what I have:
a gentle friend, a warm responsive lover.

The overture is played, the lights are down.
Now I'm the star as her directions move me.
We make the universal act our own –
a silent scene, subtitled: *Do you love me?*

The Siren and the Clown: a style of love
that suits me and is comfortable to wear,
for it's not abstract love I need prove
but the certainty of loving without fear.

There are no rules for loving or surviving
the wretched aftermath of 'getting close'.
There is no formula to balance giving
with what I get and what I have to lose.

There is no scale to measure the commitment
invested in the act of 'sleeping with':
it may be just an interim attachment,
it may revive that old 'forever' myth.

But as I play the Clown-cum-Casanova
(the only role within my repertoire),
I can believe we're more than damaged lovers –
that how we both perform is what we are.

And so, tonight, again I give my best:
we make a first night of the old routine.
The curtain falls, forever and the past
leave us to share the moment in between.

Life, the Universe…

It's the 'and everything' bit that gets me:
the numbers – of atoms in a glass of water,
grains of sand on the beach, galaxies;
the way mountains were formed; electric eels;
peacock feathers; protons and quarks;
and the questions: like did eagles' wings
evolve to be broad and long because
they soar high above the mountains,
or do they soar high above the mountains
because their wings are broad and long;
like what makes music more than just a sound;
like how did there come to be over sixty thousand
different species of slugs and snails and only
eight thousand species of birds; like…

Bonsai

I see perfection
        you see twisted, stunted growth –
            wonder if it hurts

The Punch Line

This form of life meets this other form of life,
has to decide: Can I shag it?
Can I eat it? Can it eat me?

Things evolve, although the punch line
remains pretty much the same.

This being of the genus *Homo*
meets this other being of the genus *Homo*:
they are both vegetarians which leaves
just one issue to be resolved.

They walk into a bar.

It happens all the time.

New Year 1

In hotel ballrooms or expensive clubs,
at ticket-only do's with cabaret,
or laughing through the streets from pub to pub
we drink towards the start of New Year's Day.
With no-one there to tell us when to stop
we urge each other on to self-destruction,
then one-by-one we watch each other drop
and alcohol completes her mass seduction.

The gentle morning rain can't cleanse a mess
on roads and pavements, landscaped shrubs and grass:
reminders of a night-time of excess –
the littered streamers, vomit, broken glass.

The old year's passed like piss against the wall:
retch in the new, wake sickened one and all.

Winter

frozen together
    regret takes all the duvet
        these long bitter nights

Salt of the Earth

A cruel to be
    kind of man

blunt as a scalpel

honest as an insult

open as a Spar shop

oozing sincerity like sweat
he is the salt of the earth
who would tend our wounds

The Light

I have found a tree beside the river
with a horizontal branch where I can sit
and swing my legs:
its bark is roughened but familiar
and in its trunk is a knotty hole –
a tiny litter bin for toffee papers,
lolly sticks or the foil from a choc-ice.

One evening –
the evening of another long bad day –
after I have settled with a bag of wine gums
to watch the ducks and fishermen,
I find, pushed casually into that little hole,
the wrapper from a bar of chocolate –
not one of mine.

This is more of a shock
than I could ever have imagined.

Sometimes the truth can be so blinding
that although we turn away from it
its image is reflected
off everything around us.

Relocation, Relocation, Relocation

1

mortgage advisors –
      attractive interest rates
            competitive smiles

2

single bed hovel
      would suit first-time divorcee
            or friendless loser

3

I want you to hate
      my curtains and colour scheme
            to prove you still care

The Mill

Before stone and iron and engineering brick transformed the landscape, wagtails fed and nested along the stream; songbirds in the water meadows added their voices each morning to a chorus which stretched across the county to the coast.

Then came the mills – founded on slavery, powered by poverty and steam; the cotton, picked by new world negroes being processed by spinners and weavers working for shillings into cloth to suit all of the classes: the owners in their twenty-roomed out-of-town mansions; the doctors and lawyers; the clergy and artists; the artisans, tradesmen and shopkeepers; the spinners and weavers; while coarse, cheap, checked gingham was shipped back to plantations to clothe and to colour-code the slaves who had picked it.

Now, after decades of dereliction, *The Mill is a prestige development in an urban environment: a lifestyle solution for the twenty-first century city executive* (whose third floor apartment with its open plan living space is finished in shades of terracotta and ivory with gingham soft furnishings).

Outside, the stream has been cleared of its debris and is visited sometimes by wagtails; and beyond it, a garden landscaped with shrub beds and specimen trees, is home to a blackbird which sings solo each morning with only the sound of the traffic as chorus.

And a Blackbird Sang in Portland Square

Spaced around the waiting room, we sit
attempting to maintain the symmetry
of the gaps between us as names are called
and new arrivals enter from reception.

Magazines lie scattered on the vacant seats:
What Car? Weight Watchers Magazine,
People's dog-eared Friends,
and journals which distracted readers
will only partially digest.

The Country Life is out of season:
outside it is the nicest day since winter.

*

The advice was not to worry,
but how can an imagination
fired by a single word picked from a dictionary,
not be inspired by such a subject.

The plot came instantly;
within an hour the first draft was complete;
by the morning of the first sleepless night
I had it all – the story, script and screenplay.

By now I know it word for word –
the only gap in the whole imagined manuscript
is the dialogue in the opening scene
(how do I tell them…and how will they react?)

*

I've seen her somewhere – in a shop or café?
She seems too young to be so unhappy and so pale:
I wonder if she might be pregnant –
an analogy of growth which is even more disturbing
than the bulbs and buds which wait for me outside.

A name is called –
a plain name for such a pretty girl –
she rises to leave me working on the sequel:
my sons face the complexity of manhood unsupported;
their children know me only as a photograph;
my friends have filed away my memory
having never known my full potential;
the nation's all-time favourite poem remains unwritten;
the smile of the perfect partner
I am always just about to meet
has turned to pity.

*

A blackbird sings not caring if I live or die
but still its song can soothe away the residue of fear
like the remnants of a young boy's fevered dream
beneath his mother's cooling hand.

This lovely morning greets me
with nothing more sinister than sunshine,
and if I breathe too deeply of its cool clean air
I will rise above the parked cars and the daffodils
to float outside the inward-facing offices
amazing all the clerks and County Council workers
at their first-floor windows.

But I am not an extrovert,
and so control my breathing
and submit to gravity as I walk a future
which is full of possibilities.

On a Café Terrace

In the sheltered warmth of a café terrace,
wind shuttling the clouds across the sun like shutters,
I am engaged in the company of a hen sparrow –
the most ordinary of small brown birds –
perching on the back of the opposite bench.

Head on one side, she flirts with me
as if she had been schooled in coquetry,
then hops down beside my plate
almost within the grasp of my resting hand.

The wind swoops like a hyperactive child
to play around the tables:
lifts the sparrow's feathers;
fills an empty crisp packet
sailing it across the terrace
to add its colour to a bed of flowers;
umbrellas an old man's newspaper;
frees a strand of his wife's grey hair
to fall across a cheek once smooth,
a mouth once kissed.

And I am suddenly alone
with no-one to reflect my smile.

A child runs to retrieve the litter;
the woman's face is once more aged by boredom
as her husband folds his newspaper;
the sparrow's little emptiness
is filled by crumbs of fruit cake.

Post-Its

There are people buried in my past
who are not content to rest in peace –
they reach out and haunt me.

Some leave their marks on:
    vegetarian cookery,
    most of the popular classical repertoire,
    half of the birds in Collins Field Guide.

*(your enjoyment of this ratatouille/concerto/migrating wader
is bought to you by...........)*

Others are more selective,
leaving the smallest size of yellow Post-It
with the words *remember me?*
stuck discreetly to:
    the opening bars of Shostokvich's 5th symphony,
    the sound of the first chiffchaff of spring,
    black midget gems.

Black Redstart

I saw it – a slight black bird
with a red flash of tail –
on a roof in Navigation Street.

I was seventeen, waiting for a 41
in a queue of shop and office workers
which stretched beyond the shelter,
and I wanted to use my barely broken voice
to tell them: *Look up there!*
                A bird you may never see again.

But I was a novice in a world of adults
and only spoke in answers
so I didn't even tell
the tired-looking man beside me,
who I knew from the Treasurer's Department,
I just watched, surrounded and alone,
until it flew on to a chimney then away.

At home I ticked
my Field Guide to British and European Birds:
how could I know then
that as the book became unbound and feathered,
the memory would outlive the tick;
how could I know that I would still be able to see
the small rare bird,
as clearly as on that Birmingham rooftop,
when I was as old as the man who stood beside me –
whose name I have forgotten,
who may have died
having never seen a black redstart.

Birds Don't Know it's Christmas Eve

It was always one of the bigger birds –
a solitary pigeon, a magpie or a passing crow –
landing in our garden that made me realise this.
Untouched by expectation or excitement
it would perch, or wander around, then fly away
as it would have done on any other day.

A bedraggled-looking crow trails its broken wing
around the supermarket car park.
Cars queue to enter, to park, to exit.
Stationary congas wait at the cash machines,
at the checkouts, at the cigarette and lottery counters.
With less than ten items in my basket,
I wander around, looking for organic pasta
and soya milk, as I would on any other day

New Year 2

A country walk in frosty brand new year;
a breakfast break – cold toast and thermos tea;
a jackdaw courting in a leafless tree,
watched by a jackdaw on its own and me,
    is gentle as he preens himself, then her,
not caring that we watch, he is engrossed
in love: two loners share an empty boast –
a past of pulling birds – then share my toast.

To Be

There was a blue tit
busy in a leafless bush beside the car park;
    the February sun
warming me through the windscreen;
    the smell of coffee
as I unscrewed the top of my thermos;
    the eighth item
on the standing order for my repeat prescription.

But there was no epiphany
as steam from my cup condensed against the glass;
    no enlightenment as I wondered
about the size of a blue tit's coronary arteries;
    no Hamlet moment
as the CD played Jacques Loussier;
    no option but to be

    as the blue tit busied
    and the trio played Bach
    and the sun kept shining.

Complete

A lightning flash lights up the crucifix.

In this room I first outfaced the storm,
drawing back the curtains, counting
the threat in seconds from each flash.

I am sitting on the bed I used to kneel against
to God-bless all the family:
the bed in which I would lie
in fear of unfinished homework,
with the invisible bruises of bullying
and unspeakable plans for revenge,
and with all the urgency of adolescence
(always under the eyes of Jesus).

Now there is no urgency.
I have grown out of all the old fears
and the fears that I am growing into
are still far enough away.
I have found God to be benign –
no longer trying to shame or scare me
into prayer, he leaves me alone
with my vague principles.

In the intensity of the rain-filled silences
between the crashing thunder, I find,
with this house which is no longer my home,
an unfamiliar intimacy: it recognises me
as the insecure boy it used to know
and congratulates me on my small successes.

And I know with certainty that the picture is complete:
never will my finite life be more in balance.

The storm has retreated. On the landing
my parents' bedroom door is open:
so vulnerable in their independence,
they sleep like children.

4

The Born-Again Train Spotter

Sometimes I feel quite melancholy
on a trolley on a platform at Crewe –
as I stare at the lines
I remember the times
I had so many more things to do.

I remember my teens and the sixties
when we kicked off those blue suede shoes
for a night on the town
with the new juke-box sounds
of the Mersey or rhythm and blues.

Then the Beatles and I became hippies:
oh! the parties, the pot and the girls –
I could drive them all wild
with my laid back smile
or a shake of my shoulder length curls.

Like John and Paul I was a hero
as I played my guitar in a band –
it seems so long ago,
how could I ever know
I'd end up a real Nowhere Man?

But throughout the seventies I was a star,
a success when it came to romance –
by then my technique
was almost unique
and those young girls just hadn't a chance.

But into the eighties my long hair turned grey,
and young men were making competition much harder –
they wore ten pound ties,
drove Golf Gti's,
whilst I just had flares and a Lada.

And so when the sighs changed to laughter,
when the only response was rejection,
I styled my hair,
bought new clothes to wear,
started looking in different directions.

I joined the Liberal party,
Greenpeace and Friends of the Earth;
I tried Saving the Whale,
The Campaign for Real Ale,
but I waited in vain for rebirth.

I marched and campaigned – gave up lager –
I did everything that they expected,
but my beard was too sparse,
I was of the wrong class
to ever be truly accepted,

until that 'Beer on the Pier' trip to Wigan:
we all boarded the wrong train at Crewe,
missed Wigan North Western –
the first stop was Preston
with two hours 'til the next service through.

And when some of my travelling companions
started writing down numbers of trains,
for something to do
I wrote some down too,
but since then I've just not been the same.

So I sit on this trolley and I think of the past,
of the drink and the drugs that I took –
who could have predicted
a future addicted
to trains? – but I am now, I'm hooked.

I tried to get help from a doctor,
he said it was all in my mind –
that my blatant obsession
was caused by suppression
of desires of a quite different kind.

He seemed sympathetic and eager
in explaining my psychotic complex:
he spoke about tunnels
and steam engines' funnels
in a rather unusual context.

I was lost without love on the station of life
still hoping to make a connection:
that was why, he explained,
my obsession with trains
could be cured by some female affection.

He told me of specialist agencies
who placed classified ads in the press,
and asked, if I should
find one that was good,
could I please let him have the address.

Well, I found an address in the Spotters' Gazette
that a chap on St Pancras lent me,
but I'm sorry to say
I got carried away
when I filled in the form that they sent me.

I wrote that I wanted a woman
to love me and to turn me on –
to be shamelessly mine
beside the West Coast main line
to the sound of a class 31.

I received a reply rather quickly:
my name could not be placed on their files,
they tried to be lenient
with milder deviants
but not diesel-electricophiles.

So – the joke of the nineties – I sat without love,
unashamed in an old anorak,
with my trainspotter's guide
and my pens by my side,
and my trainspotter's bag on my back.

And I'm still sitting here in the noughties,
not minding the pitying looks:
the station's my home
and I sit here alone
though I've ticked every train in my book.

I sometimes sing songs by the Beatles
when the tracks become quiet, between trains,
and imagine John Lennon,
(is there really no heaven?)
what must he think of how I have changed?

Banned from the Lonely Hearts Club,
a fool over the hill, that's me:
no more working class hero,
just a middle-aged weirdo –
but a born again spotter is something to be.

Yes, a born-again spotter is something to be.